A journey through
WALES

by

Roger Thomas

JARROLD PUBLISHING, NORWICH

INTRODUCTION

Wales is a land of many faces. Some people are attracted to its mountains, others to its coast. Those with an interest in the past talk in glowing terms about Wales's cornucopia of castles. And many are intrigued by the differences which spring from Wales's distinctive culture and deep-rooted traditions.

But we have to look even further – certainly beyond the well-known images of castles, tongue-twisting signposts and misty mountains – if we are to find the real Wales. For a start, the landscape is almost filled with mountains. Snowdon, the highest peak in Britain south of the Scottish Highlands, inevitably captures the limelight. But this rocky pinnacle is just one summit in high ground that begins at the North Wales coast and ends a stone's throw from Cardiff in the south.

The smooth, grassy flanks of the Brecon Beacons bear little similarity to Snowdon's jumbled, volcanic peaks and rock-strewn gullies. There are further upland contrasts in the wildernesses of Mid Wales, where drovers once ventured across high, featureless plateaux. And along the Wales/England border, undulating uplands and wooded valleys wear a gentle, green face.

It is also misleading to talk of Wales simply in terms of its well-known coastline. There are no less than 750 miles of Welsh seashore. The popular resorts along the sandy north coast and the Pembrokeshire coast's natural beauty are familiar to many, but they account for only about one-third of the total.

East of Pembrokeshire, for example, there are Carmarthen Bay's vast stretches of sand and the delightful Gower Peninsula. Further north, the great arc of Cardigan

Bay extends all the way to Snowdon's foothills, encompassing outstandingly beautiful estuaries and charming little resorts. And close to the bright lights of the North Wales coast resorts are the peaceful shores of the Llŷn Peninsula and Isle of Anglesey.

Wales's unparalleled scenic variety – where else can you find such vivid contrasts within such a compact area? – is mirrored elsewhere. The castles, an integral part of the country's history, are famous the world over. Grand fortresses at Caernarfon, Conwy, Harlech and Caerphilly rank amongst the finest medieval military strongholds in Europe. But again, they represent only a fraction of Wales's rich heritage.

Amongst the hundreds of castles in Wales there are mountain strongholds built by the native Welsh princes, sumptuous stately homes, and fanciful nineteenth-century 'shams' – all in addition to the fortresses built to contain the Welsh in troubled medieval times.

Heritage embraces many things. The tradition of woollen weaving still lives on, the country is dotted with craft workshops, and there are events – such as *eisteddfodau* and agricultural shows – which reflect Wales's adherence to traditional values.

But Wales has a progressive, modern side too. Anyone who has visited Cardiff or Swansea recently will testify to the cosmopolitan, forward-looking atmosphere surrounding these attractive cities. Wales is a land of many faces, as you will see from this book.

1 Sunrise high in the mountains, amongst Snowdon's jagged, rocky pinnacles

SOUTH WALES

The contrasts are more striking here than in any other part of Wales. South Wales's two 'Areas of Outstanding Natural Beauty', the Wye Valley and Gower Peninsula, epitomise this region's variety of scenery. The sheltered, lushly wooded Wye Valley snakes through idyllic border country between Monmouth and Chepstow. Gower, in complete contrast, is a bright and breezy finger of land fringed by a spectacular cliff-backed coastline.

Cardiff, Wales's elegant capital, lies on the southern coast. Its historic old waterfront is being revitalised, a process that has already given neighbouring Swansea a stunning new Maritime Quarter. Yet less than an hour's drive from the hustle and bustle of these two cities lies the Brecon Beacons National Park.

The wide, open spaces of the Brecon Beacons extend from the Wales/England border all the way across to Llandeilo. This 519-square-mile national park encompasses gloriously fresh countryside, lakes, rivers, and smooth-flanked mountains rising to almost 3,000 ft at Pen y Fan, the highest summit in South Wales. And, unexpectedly perhaps, there is more natural beauty in 'the valleys', a surprisingly green birthplace of industry.

2 The majestic ruins of Tintern Abbey, a twelfth-century religious house set in the wooded Wye Valley

3 Chepstow, Britain's first stone-built castle

4 Caerleon's Roman amphitheatre once accommodated 5,000 excited spectators

5 The pastoral lower Wye Valley, an 'Area of Outstanding Natural Beauty'

6 Cardiff's city-centre castle is a unique three-in-one historic site. The castle is part-Roman camp, part-medieval stronghold and part-Victorian mansion, the latter built with the wealth generated by the city's nineteenth-century docklands

7 The castle's ornate interior contains many treasures, including this towering fireplace in the Banqueting Hall

8 Newport's Tredegar House has a glittering interior. The seventeenth-century mansion, within the grounds of a country park, also preserves its servants' quarters and kitchens

9 Cardiff's domed City Hall fronts the city's architecturally magnificent Civic Centre, a classically inspired collection of buildings just a stone's throw from the busy shopping centre

10 Pure fantasy. Fairytale Castell Coch, on the approach to Cardiff, was built in the nineteenth century as a country retreat for the immensely wealthy Marquess of Bute, whose main home was Cardiff Castle

11 Caerphilly Castle, a 'sleeping giant' amongst medieval fortresses. Caerphilly, with its vast stone and water defences, is only now gaining recognition as one of Europe's great military sites

12 The spire and tower of Llandaff Cathedral, an ancient religious site in a quiet corner of Cardiff

13 Delicately carved love spoons were a symbol of betrothal in the rural Wales of old. This collection comes from the Welsh Folk Museum at St Fagans, Cardiff

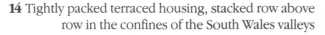

14 Tightly packed terraced housing, stacked row above row in the confines of the South Wales valleys

15 The narrow-gauge Brecon Mountain Railway runs from Merthyr Tydfil

16 Pen y Fan, the highest summit in the Brecon Beacons

17 Waterfalls between Talybont and Pontsticill

18 Swansea Marina, part of the city's new Maritime Quarter

19 Three Cliffs Bay on the Gower Peninsula. Gower's cliffs and beaches were the first part of Britain to attract 'Area of Outstanding Natural Beauty' status

20 Local seafood – including laverbread, a unique Welsh delicacy made from seaweed – on sale at Swansea Market

21 The Mumbles, a pretty sailing centre on the western approach to Swansea Bay

22 The Royal National Eisteddfod, held at a different venue each year, is Wales's most important cultural gathering

23 Perhaps the most dramatic castle in Wales, weather-beaten Carreg Cennen sits on its lonely perch in the foothills of the Black Mountain near Llandeilo

WEST WALES

The coastline, particularly the Pembrokeshire Coast National Park, is the dominant feature here. Pembrokeshire is the only coastal-based national park in Britain, and one of Europe's greatest stretches of natural seashore. The park runs for about 180 miles all the way around the south-western tip of Wales from Amroth (near Tenby) to Cardigan, extending inland along the northern coast to include the Preseli Hills.

The national park's symbol is the razorbill, a most appropriate motif for a coastline whose cliffs and islands are alive with colonies of sea-birds. And this wonderful seashore of coves, beaches, inlets and headlands is easily accessible to all, thanks to a long-distance coast footpath which runs throughout the park.

Poet Dylan Thomas observed the birds on the 'heron-priested shore' at Laugharne. This sleepy old town stands at the approach to Pembrokeshire on sandy Carmarthen Bay, a magical part of the Welsh coast that has changed little since Thomas's time. A sense of timelessness also settles over the Teifi Valley, where the farming community still gathers together on market day and the local woollen mills continue to produce traditional Welsh weaves.

24 Marloes Sands, one of Britain's most beautiful beaches, in the far west of the Pembrokeshire Coast National Park

25 Dylan Thomas's Boathouse at Laugharne is now a museum dedicated to the poet and writer

26 Tiny St Govan's Chapel, tucked in amongst the cliffs on the South Pembrokeshire coast

27 Tenby's picturesque harbour, lined with elegant Georgian houses

28 The Green Bridge of Wales, a spectacular arch carved by the sea on the cliff-backed coastline south-west of Pembroke

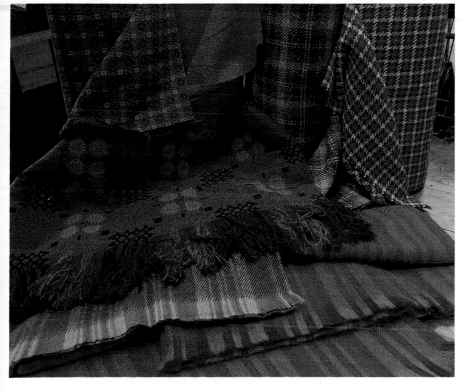

29 Mills throughout Wales continue to produce colourful Welsh weaves, some of which carry strikingly patterned Celtic designs

30 St David's Cathedral, in the smallest - and quietest - city in Britain. The cathedral is named after St David, Wales's patron saint, an early Christian leader who founded a monastic community here in the sixth century

31 The old harbour at Lower Fishguard, protected from the open seas by the sheltered waters of Fishguard Bay. Fishguard's modern ferry port is across the bay at Goodwick

32 Pentre Ifan Cromlech, near Newport. This prehistoric burial chamber is made of local 'bluestones' from the nearby Preseli Hills, an area which, despite the distance involved and problems of transportation, also provided building material for Stonehenge

33 The coracle is a one-man wicker-framed fishing boat which has been in use on Welsh rivers for at least 2,000 years. Coracle fishermen can still be seen occasionally – for example, on the River Teifi around Cenarth and Cilgerran

34 The normally sedate Teifi rushes between rocky outcrops at Cenarth Falls. This scenic spot has been popular with visitors to Wales since Victorian times

MID WALES

This is the quietest part of Wales, a sanctuary for the rare red kite, and a region which has been known to yield a nugget or two of the even rarer Welsh gold. In Mid Wales's market and country towns, the locals still go about their business much as they have always done. And the resorts along the Cardigan Bay coast are small, retaining echoes of their busy past as fishing and trading ports.

In peaceful Mid Wales the most numerous inhabitants are sheep, not people. This region is the hill-sheep farming heartland of Wales. Its remote mountains and wild moors are scattered with stone-built farmsteads, though some of this previously inaccessible upland terrain is now also occupied by forests and huge man-made lakelands.

Further east, the landscape declines into gentler hills and vales dotted with half-timbered black-and-white buildings, evidence of cross-border influences. Mid Wales's western border is the Cardigan Bay coastline, a great crescent that gives the country its distinctive 'horseshoe' shape. The bay's expansive, open seashores are a succession of grassy headlands, coves, long, sandy beaches and outstandingly beautiful estuaries.

35 The beach at Mwnt, a sheltered cove on the Cardigan Bay coast

36 Llangrannog, typical of the small coastal settlements to be found along the southern arc of Cardigan Bay

37 The unexplored hills near Cilycwm, north of Llandovery, legendary haunt of Twm Shon Cati, the Welsh Robin Hood

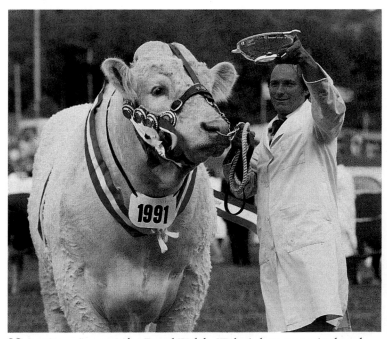

38 A prize-winner at the Royal Welsh, Wales's largest agricultural show, held each summer at Builth Wells

39 The Elan Valley reservoirs, created in remote hill country west of Rhayader at the turn of the century, were Wales's first man-made lakes

40 Holiday yachts have now replaced the trading vessels and fishing boats which used Aberaeron's harbour in the nineteenth century

41 The resort and university town of Aberystwyth, midway along Cardigan Bay, is the unofficial 'capital' of Mid Wales

42 Aberdovey, a delightfully situated little resort and sailing centre on the mouth of the Dyfi Estuary

43 Motoring at its most memorable. The Bwlch y Groes mountain road climbs high into the wildernesses above Dinas Mawddwy and Lake Vyrnwy

44 The green hills and forests around Machynlleth, in the southern reaches of the Snowdonia National Park

45 Walkers on Cader Idris, the bulky, bare-sloped mountain which rises above Dolgellau. Legend has it that those who spend a night on the summit will awake a poet or madman – or not at all . . .

46 *Above:* Dolgellau, a staunchly Welsh market town built almost entirely of the local dark stone, has an unusual architectural uniformity

47 A railway bridge with a view: BR's scenic Cambrian Coast line crosses the mouth of the Mawddach Estuary at Barmouth

48 Castle or gardens? It is difficult to choose the most attractive feature at the National Trust's Powis Castle, near Welshpool, where a sumptuous, red-stoned mansion crowns a series of Italianate terraces

49 Four-mile-long Bala Lake, the largest natural lake in Wales

50 A Gothic water tower enhances the dramatic atmosphere surrounding Lake Vyrnwy, locked away in the mountains south of Bala

51 Cwm Bychan, inland from Harlech, leads to the Rhinogs, one of the last true wildernesses in Britain

52 *Above:* Barmouth clings to the side of steep hills on the sandy mouth of the Mawddach Estuary

53 Untravelled hill, moor and forest in southern Snowdonia

54 *Above:* The end of the road. The narrow tarmac road
from Harlech into the hills goes no further than
Llyn Cwm Bychan

55 Looking northwards to the Snowdon mountain
range, which fills the skyline above Tremadog Bay

56 Harlech, on its rocky outcrop
between the mountains and the sea,
is one of the most spectacularly sited
of Wales's many medieval castles

NORTH WALES

Mount Snowdon dominates the landscape in North Wales. Its razor-sharp ridges and plunging screes fill the north-western corner of Wales, attracting outdoor enthusiasts and those who simply want to gaze at savagely beautiful mountain scenery. The mountain gives its name to the 845-square-mile Snowdonia National Park, whose boundaries extend well beyond Snowdon itself to encompass the lofty reaches above Bala Lake and the highlands as far south as Machynlleth in Mid Wales.

Snowdonia's eastern boundary is the sheltered Vale of Conwy. From here, a lower landscape of hills, vales and moors rolls away to the Wales/England border, with a final flourish along the hump-backed Clwydian Hills, an 'Area of Outstanding Natural Beauty'.

People have been visiting the North Wales coast ever since the seaside holiday first became fashionable. Llandudno, the undisputed 'Queen of the Coast', retains all the style of its Victorian and Edwardian past. In quiet contrast there are two more 'Areas of Outstanding Beauty' – the cliff-backed Llŷn Peninsula and the sandy bays of the Isle of Anglesey.

57 The Traeth Bach sands, where the waters of the Dwyryd and Glaslyn rivers flow into Tremadog Bay

58 Portmeirion, created by architect Sir Clough Williams-Ellis, surely ranks amongst the world's strangest villages. Visitors to this beguiling, bizarre village could be forgiven for thinking that they had suddenly been transported from North Wales to southern Italy

59 Porthmadog, now a popular sailing centre, grew up as a slate-exporting port

60 Criccieth is guarded by its sturdy little castle

61 The tip of the Llŷn Peninsula, the wildly beautiful 'Land's End of North Wales'

62 Just south of Beddgelert, the Glaslyn rushes through the shady, steep-sided Aberglaslyn Pass

63 Bardsey Island, off the western tip of the Llŷn Peninsula. Pilgrims once made the difficult crossing to Bardsey, the 'Isle of 20,000 Saints', where a monastic community was founded in the seventh century

64 The River Ogwen flows through rugged uplands on its short trip from Snowdonia to the sea

65 Looking towards Snowdon from Capel Curig. The mountain gives its name to the 845-square-mile Snowdonia National Park, a huge expanse of upland extending southwards into the heart of Mid Wales

66 Mountaineering made easy, by riding the train to the top of Snowdon. The narrow-gauge railway takes about an hour to climb the 4½ miles from Llanberis to within a short distance of the 3,560-ft summit

67 Llyn Padarn and Llyn Peris on the approach to the Llanberis Pass. Hidden deep within the mountainside to the right are the tunnels and turbines of the mammoth Dinorwig Hydro-electricity Pumped Storage Scheme

68 Sunset over Snowdonia

69 An old pack-horse bridge across the River Lledr near Betws-y-coed

70 Boulder-strewn mountain slopes
along Snowdonia's Nant Ffrancon Pass

71 The Swallow Falls, Betws-y-coed,
a famous North Wales beauty spot

72 Thomas Telford's elegant Menai Suspension Bridge links the Isle of Anglesey to mainland Wales

73 Caernarfon Castle, Wales's best-known medieval fortress

74 Caernarfon was constructed in the thirteenth century by the English king Edward I, as one of his 'iron ring' of fortresses around Snowdonia built to subdue the Welsh. Caernarfon's imperious character is no accident – the castle was designed to serve as a royal palace as well as military stronghold

75 The huge sweep of sands along Llanddwyn Bay on the Isle of Anglesey

76 Anglesey's Plas Newydd, a splendid mansion in the care of the National Trust, stands in beautiful grounds overlooking the Menai Strait

77 The port of Holyhead is busy with
fishing boats and Irish Sea ferries

78 Beaumaris Castle, begun in 1295 but never completed, was the last – and most sophisticated – Edwardian fortress to be built in Wales

81 Of all the Edwardian fortresses in North Wales, mighty Conwy Castle retains the most authentic spirit of medieval times amongst its ancient walls and soaring towers

79 Penrhyn Castle, Bangor, is an elaborate 'sham'. This National Trust property was constructed in convincing neo-Norman style for a nineteenth-century slate magnate

80 The graceful crescent of sand and seafront at Llandudno, neatly framed between the Great and Little Orme headlands

82 The formal lily pond at the National Trust's Bodnant Garden, in the Conwy Valley near Llandudno

83 Square-towered Dolwyddelan Castle, a stronghold of the Welsh princes, stands guard over a mountain pass in deepest Snowdonia

84 Ruthin is an architectural gem. Its streets and narrow lanes are filled with half-timbered black-and-white dwellings and fine Georgian houses

85 Erddig, near Wrexham, was rescued from slow decline by the National Trust in the 1970s. It gives visitors a fascinating glimpse into the 'upstairs, downstairs' life on a country estate of old

86 The art of the iron craftsman. These gates, made by the celebrated Davies brothers of Bersham between 1719 and 1721, stand at the entrance to the National Trust's Chirk Castle

87 Llangollen's International Eisteddfod is a colourful, cosmopolitan affair. Founded in 1947 as a contribution to world peace, the annual summer festival attracts musicians and dancers from many countries

89 Llangollen stands at the gateway to North Wales, where the English lowlands funnel into a lovely valley enclosed by rolling, green hills

88 Plas Newydd was the home of the eccentric 'Ladies of Llangollen' in the eighteenth and early nineteenth centuries

90 Pistyll Rhaeadr, Wales's highest waterfall, hidden in the hills near Llanrhaeadr ym Mochnant

Front cover: Llyn Gwynant in the shadow of Snowdon, the highest mountain in England and Wales

Title page: Llyn Ogwen in the heart of the Snowdonia National Park

Back cover: Carreg Cennen Castle, perched on its crag overlooking the Black Mountain near Llandeilo

Text by Roger Thomas
ISBN 0-7117-0510-0
© Jarrold Publishing 1990
Published by Jarrold Publishing, Norwich. Printed in Wales. 1/90
Acknowledgements
The publishers are grateful to the Wales Tourist Board for their assistance with this book.

Photo credits National Trust: **title page**, **48**, **61**, **76**, **79**, **85**; CADW – Welsh Historic Monuments: **3**, **60**, **78**; Rex Moreton: **8**; Douglas Hardy: **23**, **34**; Ronald Thompson: **64**, **74**, **81**; Mike Cullen: **68**; G.B. Allsop: **69**; Wales Tourist Board/Jarrold Publishing: **all others.**